Animals in Ancient Egypt

Written by Abbie Rushton
Illustrated by Josy Bloggs

Contents

Greetings from Miu! 3
Introducing ancient Egypt 4
Cats 8
Dogs 10
Crocodiles 12
Birds 14
How do we know? 16
Scarab beetles 18
Hippos 20
Animal mummies 22
Glossary and Index 24

OXFORD
UNIVERSITY PRESS

Words to look out for ...

inspiration NOUN
If someone or something is an inspiration, or gives you inspiration, they encourage you or fill you with ideas.

investigate VERB
To investigate something is to find out as much as you can about it.

practical ADJECTIVE
Something is practical when it is likely to be useful.

predict VERB
To predict something is to say that it will happen in the future.

respond VERB
To respond to someone or something is to reply or react to them.

secure ADJECTIVE
Something that is secure is safe or protected from attack.

Greetings from Miu!

Hello – I am Miu. My name means 'cat' in Ancient Egyptian. It also sounds like the sound I make: 'mew'!

In this book, we will <u>investigate</u> animals in Ancient Egypt.

To <u>investigate</u> something is to find out as much as you can about it.

Introducing ancient Egypt

Egypt is a country in north Africa. Its capital city is Cairo. The River Nile runs through the country.

The Nile

The River Nile is the main river in Egypt. People began to live near the Nile about 9000 years ago. The river had many practical uses. It provided water for:

- growing crops
- drinking
- washing
- transport.

Something is practical when it is likely to be useful.

The pyramids

The ancient Egyptians built pyramids as **tombs** for kings and queens.

Some pyramids are more than 4500 years old. Many of them are still standing today. I don't think the builders could have predicted that!

modern Cairo

ancient pyramid

To predict something is to say that it will happen in the future.

Ancient beliefs

Ancient Egyptians believed in lots of gods. Their gods often had animal heads.

The **roles** of these gods were often similar to something their animal did.

Look out for fact boxes that explain more about their gods!

Purr-fect pets!

Ancient Egyptians loved to keep pets! Just like us, they were sad when their pets died. To show this, if a cat died, the ancient Egyptians responded by shaving their eyebrows. For dogs, they responded by shaving all of their body hair!

This wall painting shows a cat under its owner's chair. It has been given a fish!

To respond to someone or something is to reply or react to them.

Cats

Ancient Egyptians loved cats. Their cats caught pests like rats, mice and snakes.

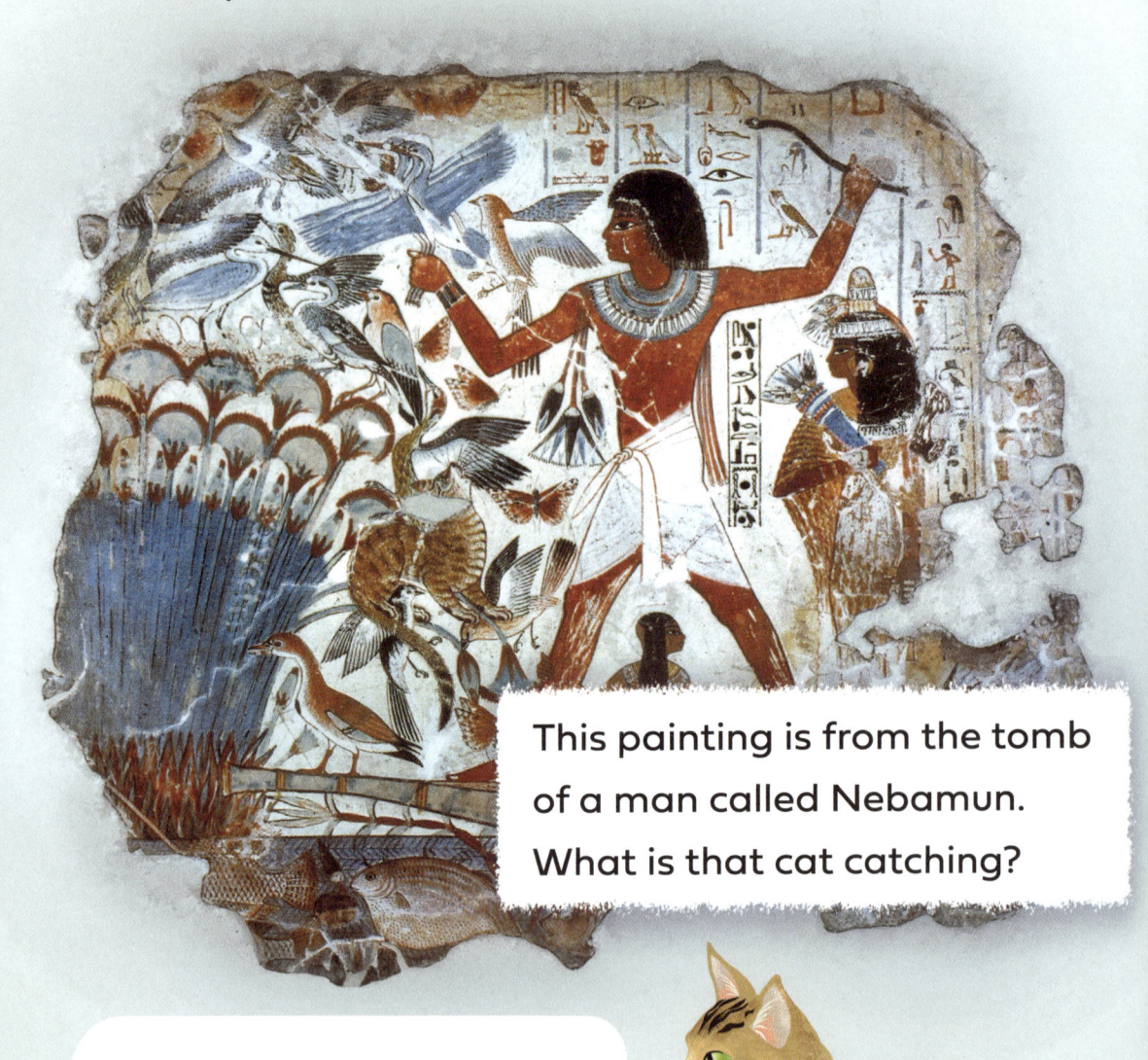

This painting is from the tomb of a man called Nebamun. What is that cat catching?

Some ancient Egyptians even dressed their cats in jewellery!

Ancient Egyptians thought cats brought good luck. When their owners died, cats were often buried with them.

Name: Bastet

Animal: cat's head

Goddess of: good health, safety and the home

Role: keeping homes secure

This cat was **carved** in gold!

Something that is secure is safe or protected from attack.

9

Dogs

Dogs were used for hunting and guarding homes. Ancient Egyptians walked their dogs on leads, just like people do now.

The ancient Egyptian word for 'dog' was 'iwiw'. They might have taken inspiration from the sound of a dog's bark!

A wall painting shows an ancient Egyptian walking their dog – and a mongoose!

If someone or something is an inspiration, or gives you inspiration, they encourage you or fill you with ideas.

Can you spot the owner's dog in this carving?

Name: Anubis

Animal: dog's head

God of: dead people

Role: helping with burials

Crocodiles

Lots of crocodiles live near the River Nile. Ancient Egyptians were afraid of crocodiles. The crocodiles were very dangerous and attacked people.

Ancient Egyptians also respected crocodiles. They were strong and powerful hunters.

Name: Sobek

Animal: crocodile's head

God of: creation

Role: looking after the army and the Nile; creating the world

The ancient Egyptians hunted crocodiles to give as gifts to the gods. They also kept them in pools or **temples**.

This was a temple for Sobek.

These crocodiles were buried in their temple when they died.

Birds

Ancient Egyptians thought birds could fly close to the gods.

The falcon was an important bird in ancient Egypt. It was a powerful hunter. Experts think some Ancient Egyptians kept falcons for hunting.

This is a statue of a falcon. It is wearing the Double Crown of Egypt.

There were several gods who looked like birds.

Thoth had the head of an ibis (a kind of water bird).

Ra had the head of a falcon.

Nekhbet (say: nek-bet) had a vulture's head.

Name: Horus

Animal: falcon's head

God of: war and the sky

Role: protecting rulers; watching over battles

a temple for Horus

How do we know?

So, how do we know about ancient Egyptians?

Hieroglyphs

Ancient Egyptians used pictures called hieroglyphs (say: high-ro-gliffs) to write. Some hieroglyphs have survived on paper. Some are carved in stone. Some are painted on walls. Animals were often used in hieroglyphs.

= F

= M

= L

Wall art

Lots of wall carvings and paintings survive. Many of them show animals. This tells us how important animals were.

Baboons were another important animal. In this painting, there is one baboon for each hour of the night.

Scarab beetles

In Egypt, there is a type of beetle called a scarab. Scarabs collect balls of dung – that's animal droppings!

They roll the balls and bury them underground. The ancient Egyptians thought this seemed like the sun being rolled across the sky.

This bracelet shows a scarab pushing the sun.

Scarab beetles were linked to the sun, which gives warmth and helps crops grow. This meant scarabs were very important.

Kings were buried with scarab beetle jewellery.

Name: Khepri

Animal: scarab head

God of: the sun

Role: pushing the sun across the sky

Which piece of scarab jewellery do you like most?

Hippos

Hippos are **extinct** in Egypt today. That is partly because ancient Egyptians hunted them. They thought killing hippos was a way to show strength.

a hippo hunting

river

However, ancient Egyptians also respected hippos. Hippos can go underwater and come up again. Ancient Egyptians thought this was like being born again.

This hippo statue is painted with river plants.

Female hippos are fierce protectors of their children. The ancient Egyptians may have been responding to this fact when they made their goddess of **motherhood** part hippo. She was also part crocodile and part lion!

Name: Taweret

Animal: hippo's body, crocodile's tail, lion's legs

Goddess of: mothers

Role: helping women in childbirth

To respond to someone or something is to reply or react to them.

Animal mummies

The ancient Egyptians wanted their bodies to be secure inside their pyramids. So they wrapped bodies in bandages. This was called mummification. It kept the bodies safe.

This painting shows the god Anubis mummifying a king.

Something that is secure is safe or protected from attack.

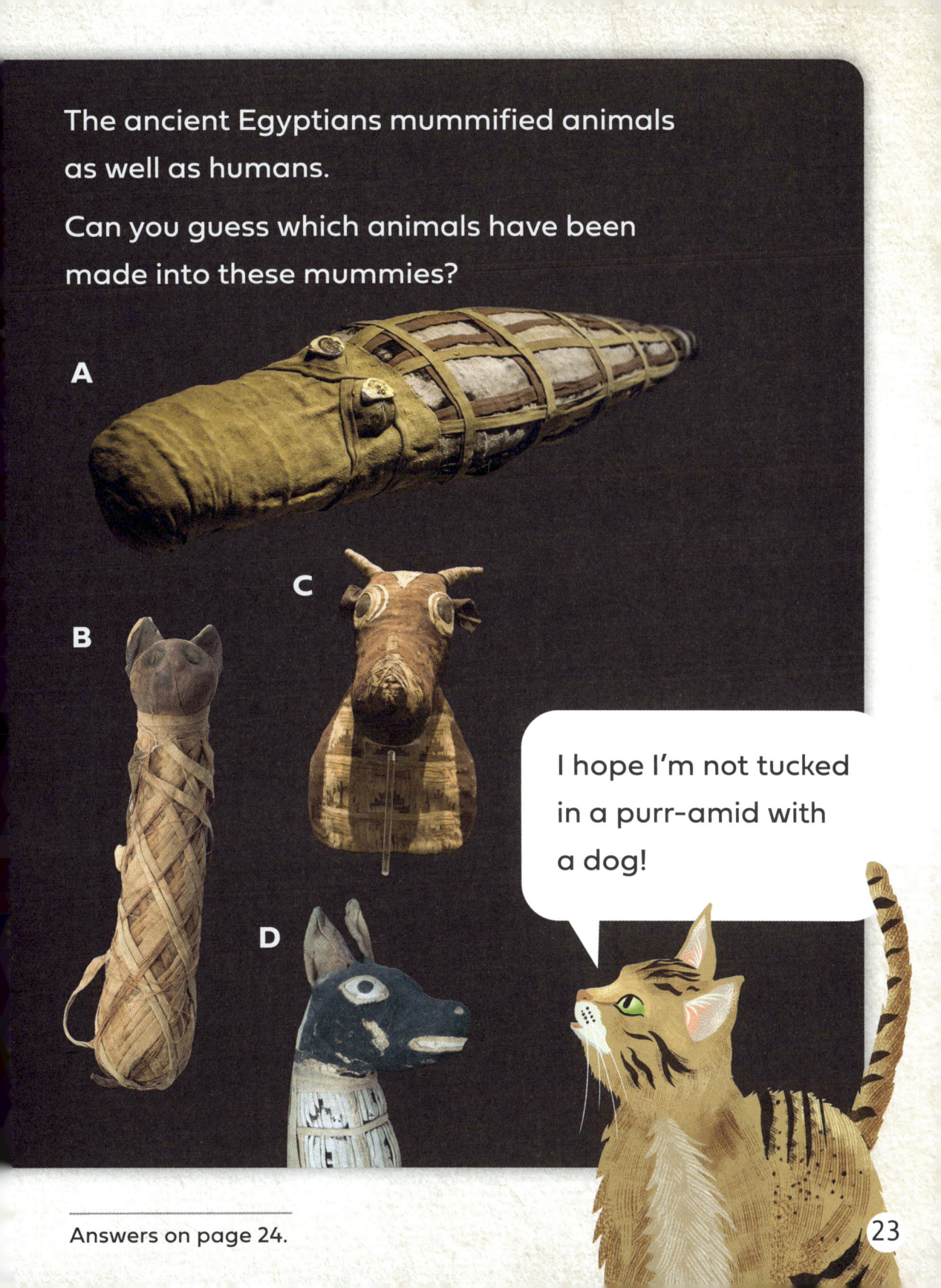

The ancient Egyptians mummified animals as well as humans.

Can you guess which animals have been made into these mummies?

A

B

C

D

I hope I'm not tucked in a purr-amid with a dog!

Answers on page 24.

23

Glossary

carved: made by cutting into something

creation: the action of making something from the start

extinct: if an animal is extinct, there are none of that animal still alive

motherhood: being a mother

role: what you are for, or supposed to do

temples: a temple is a place where people can feel close to their god or gods

tomb: a place where a person is buried after they have died

Index

Ancient Egyptian gods	6, 9, 11, 13, 15, 19, 21
hieroglyphs	16
Nile	4, 12–13
pyramids	5, 22
wall art	7, 8, 10, 16–17

mummified animals: A. crocodile, B. cat, C. cow, D. dog